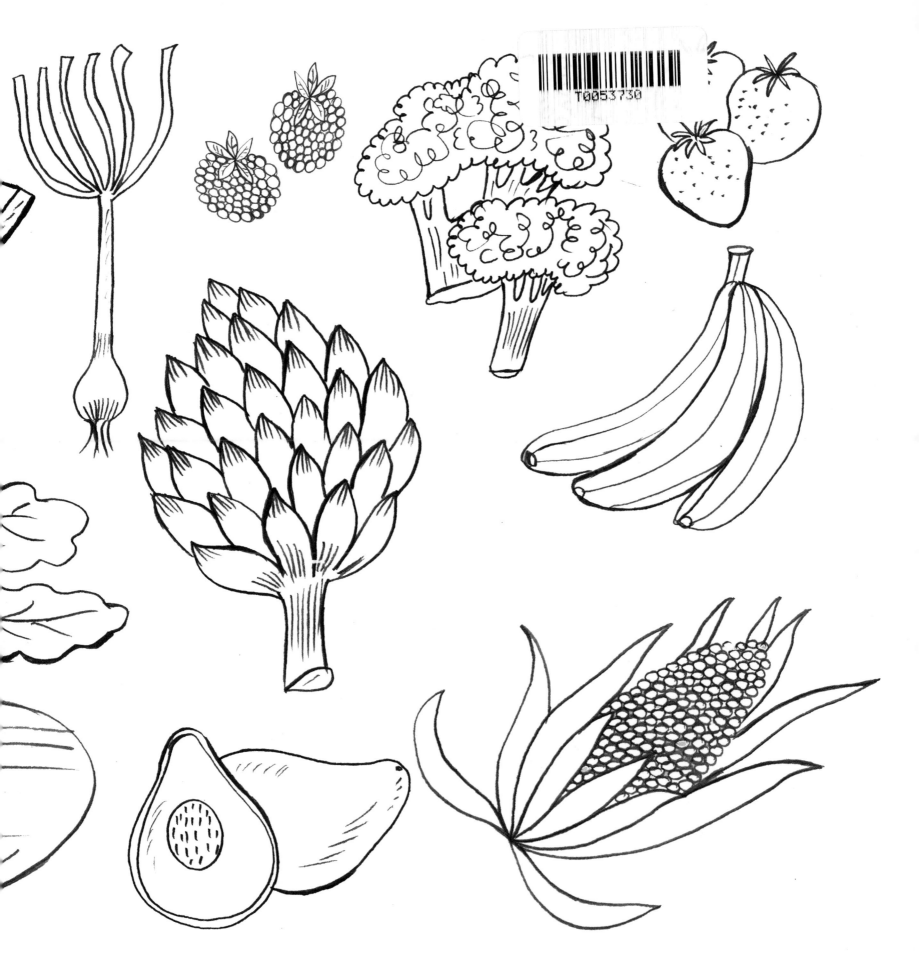

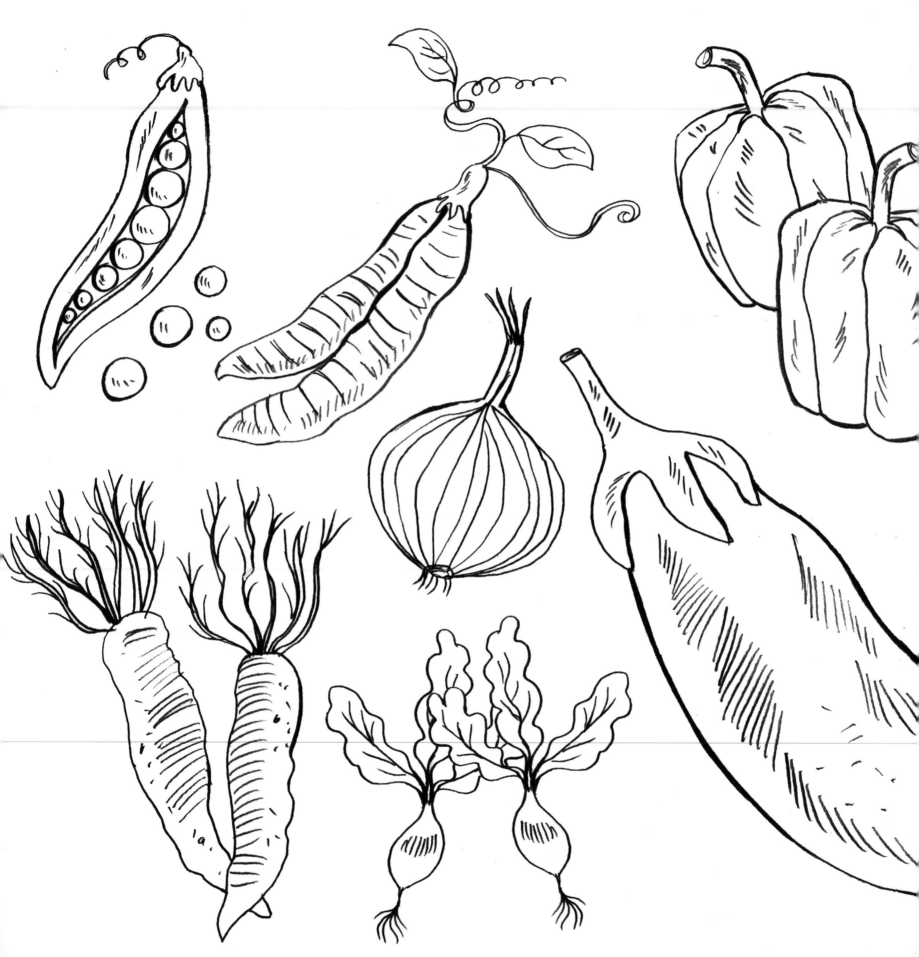

PRAISE FOR *HOW DOES OUR FOOD GROW?*

"Not only is *How Does Our Food Grow?* a delightful book to read, but it also educates young readers and offers delicious recipes that the whole family will enjoy preparing and sharing. I am sure it will be treasured by children from all around the world."

H.E. AMBASSADOR JOSÉ BLANCO,
THE PERMANENT MISSION OF THE DOMINICAN REPUBLIC TO THE UNITED NATIONS

"What a great book! Whether you're a curious child, an interested parent, a climate diplomat, or a passionate foodie, you'll enjoy discovering the world of food and learn how we cultivate and consume our food sustainably. *How Does Our Food Grow?* is a colorful, fun, and educational book about one of the essential aspects of our lives. A feast for the eyes, nutrition for the brain, and a must-read for young and old."

H.E. AMBASSADOR ALEXANDER MARSCHIK,
THE PERMANENT MISSION OF AUSTRIA TO THE UNITED NATIONS

"This book should be in every home, every library, and every classroom to teach our children how the food they eat affects their bodies and the planet. *How Does Our Food Grow?* aims at encouraging curiosity and responsibility around our food choices and practices from a young age."

H.E. AMBASSADOR PIO WENNUBST, THE PERMANENT MISSION OF SWITZERLAND
TO THE FOOD AND AGRICULTURE ORGANIZATION OF THE UNITED NATIONS

"Along with ensuring all children have access to a nutritious meal at school, The School Meals Coalition seeks to foster an understanding of food and healthy and sustainable behaviours that can extend beyond school, and into children's families and communities throughout their lives. *How Does Our Food Grow?* is a helpful tool in this educational process as it reinforces healthy food habits in a fun, visual, and relatable way."

SCHOOL MEALS COALITION,
AN INITIATIVE OF GOVERNMENTS SUPPORTED BY THE UNITED NATIONS WORLD FOOD PROGRAMME

FAMILIUS

Published by Familius LLC, www.familius.com
PO Box 1249, Reedley, CA 93654

Familius books are available at special discounts for bulk purchases,
whether for sales promotions or for family or corporate use. For more information,
contact Familius Sales at orders@familius.com.

Library of Congress Control Number: 2022950527

Print ISBN 978-1-64170-991-0
Ebook ISBN 978-1-64170-909-5
KF 978-1-64170-981-1
FE 978-1-64170-980-4

Printed in China with sustainable materials

Edited by Earlene Cruz, Sara Bond, Lauren Salkeld, and Peg Sandkam
Cover and book design by Brooke Jorden
Map elements sourced from Shutterstock.com

10 9 8 7 6 5 4 3 2 1

First Edition

HOW DOES OUR FOOD GROW?

BROOKE JORDEN with

ILLUSTRATED BY
KAY WIDDOWSON

FRUITS AND VEGETABLES all taste great,
but how did they end up on your plate?
The fresh and colorful foods you know
came from farms—that's where they grow!
Some grow underground and some hang from trees.
Can you find them all? Let's look and see!

Different fruits and vegetables grow
all over the world. What have you seen
growing where you live?

APPLES come in all colors and sizes.

Some sweet, some tart—a bushel of surprises!

They grow on trees, strong and tall,

then we pick them before they fall.

Pears and figs come from orchards too.

Find them 'round the world—from China to Peru!

Did you know that there are hundreds of varieties of apples grown around the world? How many different kinds have you tried?

ZUCCHINI grows well in sunshine and heat.
Its flavor simply can't be beat!
Under wide, flat leaves you will find
zucchini grows on a thick green vine.
Vines grow lots of our favorite eats,
like watermelon, pumpkin, and other treats.

Did you know you can even eat the flower of the zucchini plant? Fried squash blossoms are very popular in Italy.

STRAWBERRIES are red and sweet.
Where do they grow? Watch your feet!
They grow on forbs close to the ground:
some are heart-shaped and others more round.
All berries are yummy AND good for your brain,
but be careful—the colorful juice might stain!

Fruits and vegetables do not have to have a perfect shape to be delicious. In fact, no matter the shape of your strawberries, apples, or carrots, they will give you the same nutrients. So next time you visit a market, give a funny-looking fruit a try!

How does **CORN** grow? Up high on a stalk!
Corn has "ears," but it can't talk.
Another name for corn is "maize."
People eat it worldwide in different ways.
While corn on the cob is a vegetable,
popcorn is considered a grain at your table.

Grains need less water to grow than other
kinds of food, so they are good for the
environment and for our bodies!

There are other stalks that you can eat.
They grow in bunches, tall and neat.
ASPARAGUS grows from a rhizome root,
a springtime crown that sprouts up tender shoots.
These tasty spears are packed with vitamin C.
They can be purple or white, but are usually green.

Did you know there is a recipe for cooking asparagus in the world's oldest surviving cookbook? This means that people have been eating asparagus for a very long time!

Another rhizome for your lunch:
BANANAS grow in a crowded bunch.
They start out green and change to yellow.
Bananas are sweet, and plantains are more mellow.
A banana's strong skin is a natural box,
so you don't need extra packaging—and that totally rocks!

Because bananas are rich in nutrients, including potassium, they are eaten all around the world. In India, kids love banana fritters called *gulgule*. In the United States, frozen bananas are a popular treat. In Venezuela, they fry and eat the peel! How does your family eat bananas?

For cousins **BROCCOLI** and **CAULIFLOWER**,
our favorite part to eat is actually a flower.
Those flower-bud clusters and tree-like stalks
are the signature style of Mr. Broc.
Broccoli plants can't take the heat,
so plant when it's cool and you're in for a treat.

Broccoli and cauliflower are called "cruciferous" vegetables.
You can eat them raw, cooked, with dip, or in soups and curries.
What is your favorite way to eat broccoli?

Mashed into guacamole or on top of toast,
this tropical fruit is a favorite for most.
AVOCADOS are packed with healthy fats, grow on a tree,
and have a pit in the middle—just like lychee.
With a tough, bumpy outside and creamy insides to share,
some people call it an "alligator pear."

It takes an avocado tree 3–5 years to grow its first
fruit. But after that, they produce avocados every
year! Avocados are delicious and nutritious, and a
perfect fruit for babies just learning to eat solid foods.

A prickly **PINEAPPLE** has a secret to hide:
sweet yellow juicy goodness inside!
They first grew in the rainforests of Brazil,
where wise local farmers still harvest them with skill.
Pineapples love climates with a tropical breeze,
sunshine, rain, and tall palm trees.

The original name of a pineapple is *ananas comosus*; this is Guarani for "fragrant and excellent fruit." The pineapple got its name in English because European explorers thought it looked like a pinecone.

Their tops peeking out from underground,
beneath the soil, what surprises can be found?
POTATOES grown in tidy rows
give us energy and help us grow.
From hashed to mashed to sweet potato pie,
you've got to give different potatoes a try!

Did you know there are more than 4000 species
of potatoes grown in the Andes Mountains in
South America? Potatoes come in white, orange,
purple, among other colors, and can grow well in a
variety of climates and on almost every continent.

We love to eat legumes, especially **BEANS**.
Serve them with rice for a complete protein!
Edamame, black beans, soy, or chickpeas,
pinto or kidney beans—more? Yes, please!
And one more "bean" we can't forget:
cacao beans give us chocolate!

The beans, peas, and lentils we eat—called "pulses"—are the seeds of legume plants. They give us protein and energy, but they require less water and fuel from the earth to grow than other plants.

Here we have another bean.

This one is quite long and green.

The beans, pods, and leaves all have a nice taste.

When you eat the whole thing, nothing goes to waste.

GREEN BEANS grow quickly and are gentle on soil.

Freeze for later or try them seasoned and broiled!

Green beans have fun names in different countries: runner beans, strong beans, snake beans, and long beans! Do you like to eat them crunchy or soft?

Sometimes food is shipped over land and sea,
but we can also choose to eat locally.
Markets and food stands have a rainbow of choices,
and farmers, your neighbors, are wise local voices.
Whether it's yuzu, lentils, or pomegranate,
eating food grown nearby is good for you and the planet.

Have you ever met a farmer? What is
one question you would want to ask the
farmer who grows your food?

Eating for a Healthier Planet and a Happier You!

from The Kitchen Connection Alliance

TERMS TO KNOW

CULTIVATING: Preparing and using land for farming

FORB: Any herb other than grass

FRUIT: A sweet and fleshy part of a tree that contains seeds and can be eaten

HARVEST: Collecting fruits or vegetables to be eaten

HUSK: A dry outer shell that covers some fruits and vegetables (such as corn!)

HEALTHY DIET: A diet that has the right amount and the right kinds of food so that we can have the energy to do everyday activities. To have a healthy diet, we should aim to eat a variety of fruits and vegetables!

ORCHARD: A piece of land, normally far from surrounding land, in which fruit trees are grown

RHIZOME: A horizontal stem of a plant that is usually found underground, often sending out roots and shoots from its nodes. Some plants have rhizomes that grow above ground or that sit at the soil surface. Rhizomes may also be referred to as creeping rootstalks.

STALK: The stem or main axis of a plant

VEGETABLE: A plant or part of a plant that we can eat

VITAMINS: The important parts of the food we eat that are essential for growing and staying healthy

Sharing meals with family and friends helps us feel connected, healthy, and happy. The foods we learned about in this book grow in unique ways all over the world and taste delicious—but they have other special qualities too. Because there are now over eight billion people on the planet, we have to produce a lot of food! The types of foods we choose to produce can help protect against climate change, keep our communities healthy, reduce waste, promote sustainability, and preserve our natural environment. Keep reading to find out how!

CLIMATE CHANGE

—Just like people, plants need the right conditions to grow. Sunshine, water, and healthy soil are important for plants, but the amount of each that they get needs to be just right. For example: pineapples thrive in tropical breezy climates and zucchini needs lots of sunshine and heat, but broccoli can't grow where it's too hot! If our climate changes, the kinds of fruits and vegetables we can grow changes too. Take a look around you . . . what conditions make YOU feel your best?

COMMUNITY HEALTH

–Our story showed how beautiful markets and food stands are, but their rainbow of fruits, vegetables, and friendly faces are more than just pretty! The foods for sale are full of nutrients that can help us grow stronger and smarter. Foods have nutritional building blocks like protein, carbohydrates, fat, vitamins, and minerals—and we need all of them to support loving hearts, clever minds, and healthy bodies. Trying lots of different foods makes sure we have all the nutritional building blocks we need (the greater diversity is better for us—the planet—and it tastes great too!).

REDUCING FOOD WASTE

–Bananas, apples, and green beans have natural "packaging" thanks to their skin. Can you think of any other foods that don't need a wrapper? When we choose foods that don't need extra packaging, we reduce the amount of waste produced by food stores and households. Producing less waste helps protect the environment and keeps our communities clean!

–Sometimes we get to eat the WHOLE food, skin and all! Remember zucchini? The skin, flesh, and seeds are edible, so nothing gets thrown away when we use it for food. Another way to reduce food waste is looking for silly shapes at the grocery store: can you find lumpy potatoes, or apples shaped like ovals? No matter what a food looks like, its energy and taste are the same. Choosing the silly shapes keeps them from being forgotten about and thrown away.

SUSTAINABLE CONSUMPTION AND PRODUCTION

–How many ways can you think of to prepare cranberries? While we can enjoy them when they're fresh, they can also be baked into a pie, dehydrated to sprinkle on rice, or frozen to use later. Learning how to save and enjoy foods all year long helps us eat more sustainably. In fact, lots of food can last longer if stored properly or frozen! Have you heard of canning, pickling, or fermenting? All of these are ways to make food last longer.

–Another way we can eat sustainably is choosing foods that are grown near where we live and are "in season." Farmers practice sustainability by planting different crops during different parts of the year and choosing foods that grow best in their climate. When we eat these foods, it supports the farmers and strengthens our communities.

PLANETARY HEALTH AND BIODIVERSITY

–The foods in this book aren't just tasty and healthy for people. They're healthy for the planet too! Grains, vegetables, and fruits need less water to grow than other kinds of food. Water is one of Earth's most precious resources, so it's important to save as much of it as we can.

–Plant foods are also gentle on the soil. Have you ever looked closely at the soil where you live? Can you find small bugs, worms, or different colors? Is it moist or dry? Soil delivers nutrients to plants, and when the plants are gentle on it, it can continue delivering nutrients for many years.

–When the soil is healthy, lots of different kinds of crops can flourish. Just like the world is better because of diverse people, our planet is better with diverse plants! Remember: we learned that there are more than 4000 different kinds of potatoes . . . that's a LOT! How many kinds of potatoes have you tried?

On the following pages, enjoy recipes selected from *The Cookbook in Support of the United Nations: For People and Planet.* Each recipe uses ingredients you learned about in this book.

GARBANZOS CON ESPINACAS

Moorish-Style Chickpea and Spinach Stew

José Andrés
Spain

¼ cup (60 ml) extra-virgin olive oil, preferably Spanish

6 garlic cloves, peeled

2 ounces (56 g) sliced white bread, crusts removed (1 to 2 slices)

2 tablespoons pimentón

1 pinch saffron threads, preferably Spanish

1 teaspoon ground cumin

2 tablespoons sherry vinegar

2 (14-ounce / 400 g) cans chickpeas (do not drain)

½ pound (225 g) spinach

Kosher salt and freshly ground white pepper

Crusty bread, for serving

In a small frying pan, heat the oil over medium-low heat. Add the garlic and cook, stirring, until browned, about 3 minutes. Remove the garlic from the pan and set it aside. Working in batches as needed, add the bread to the pan and brown it on both sides, about 1 minute per side. Remove the bread from the pan and set it aside. Do not clean the pan.

Using a mortar and pestle, smash the browned garlic and toasted bread into a very thick paste.

Once the pan used to cook the garlic and bread has cooled for a few minutes, add the pimentón, saffron and cumin, followed by the sherry vinegar. Stir to combine and set the pan aside.

In a medium saucepan, bring the chickpeas and their liquid to a low boil over medium heat. Add the spinach and a little water as needed if there's not enough liquid to cook the spinach. Simmer for 5 minutes and then add the pimentón mixture, along with the garlic-bread paste, and stir to combine—you should have a thick, stew-like sauce.

Continue simmering until the chickpeas are soft and flavorful, about 5 more minutes. Season with salt and white pepper and serve hot with crusty bread.

INGREDIENT SPOTLIGHT

beans (chickpeas)

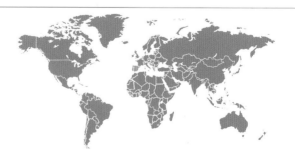

Carbon Emissions: CO2e: 0.19

This meal emits 81.85 percent less carbon than the average meal in the world's highest-emitting countries.

BEAN AND BELL PEPPER CHILI
with Cauliflower Rice

Gunhild Stordalen
Norway

4 tablespoons (60 ml) canola oil

1 large white onion, cut into large chunks

1 red bell pepper, cut into large chunks

1 green bell pepper, cut into large chunks

Salt and freshly ground black pepper

2 garlic cloves, finely chopped

1 to 2 fresh red chilis, finely chopped

1 small cinnamon stick

1 teaspoon ground coriander

2 teaspoons ground cumin

2 teaspoons paprika

2 to 3 teaspoons chili powder

½ pound (225 g) cremini mushrooms, halved

1 (14.5-ounce / 425 g) can diced tomatoes and their juices

1 ¾ cups (420 ml) vegetable broth

2 tablespoons tomato paste

1 tablespoon brown sugar or honey

2 (14-ounce / 400 g) cans red kidney beans, drained and washed

1 head cauliflower, trimmed and cut into florets

1 ½ ounces (42 g) dark chocolate (at least 70%), grated or finely chopped, plus more for serving

Chopped fresh flat-leaf cilantro (coriander) leaves, for serving

Yogurt or sour cream, for serving

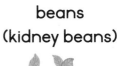

In a large Dutch oven, heat 2 tablespoons of the canola oil over medium-high heat. Add the onion, red and green bell peppers and a pinch of salt and cook, stirring often, until the onion and peppers are soft, about 10 minutes. Add the garlic, fresh red chili, cinnamon stick, coriander, cumin, paprika and chili powder and cook, stirring, until fragrant, 1 to 2 minutes. Add the mushrooms, toss to coat in the spices and cook, stirring, for 2 minutes. Add the diced tomatoes and their juices, the vegetable broth, tomato paste, brown sugar and a generous pinch of salt. Bring to a boil and then cover, reduce the heat to medium-low and gently simmer for 10 minutes. Add the kidney beans and continue gently simmering for about 30 minutes to heat the beans and thicken the chili slightly.

Meanwhile, make the cauliflower rice. Working in batches as needed, in a food processor, pulse the cauliflower until it resembles rice or couscous-sized granules.

When the chili is done, in a large frying pan, heat the remaining 2 tablespoons of canola oil over medium-high heat. Add the cauliflower rice and cook, tossing often, until heated through and browned in some places, about 5 minutes. Season with salt and pepper.

Just before serving, remove the cinnamon stick from the chili and add the chocolate. Sprinkle with fresh cilantro and more chocolate and serve with the cauliflower rice and yogurt or sour cream on the side.

INGREDIENT SPOTLIGHT

**beans
(kidney beans)**

cacao

cauliflower

*Carbon Emissions:
CO2e: 0.7*

This meal emits 33.14 percent less carbon than the average meal in the world's highest-emitting countries.

ON SIKIL BI BU'UL

Black Bean Pipian

Rosalia Chay Chuc
Mayan Community
Mexico

1 cup (190 g) dried black beans, picked over and rinsed

1 large head garlic

1 teaspoon olive oil

⅓ cup (56 g) whole annatto seeds (achiote)

1 tablespoon dried Mexican oregano

½ tablespoon freshly ground black pepper

¼ cup (40 g) pepitas (toasted pumpkin seeds)

1 ½ teaspoons salt

Chopped red onion, fresh cilantro (coriander) and warm corn tortillas, for serving

In a large bowl, combine the black beans with enough room temperature water to cover. Let stand for at least 8 hours or over-night. Drain the beans and discard the water.

Preheat the oven to 400°F (200°C).

Peel any loose papery skins off the head of garlic, then cut about a ¼ inch (0.5 cm) off the top to expose the individual cloves. Place the head of garlic on a piece of aluminum foil and drizzle with the olive oil. Wrap the foil around the head of garlic, place on a sheet pan or in a small baking dish, and roast until the cloves closest to the center are completely soft when pierced with a knife, 40 to 50 minutes. Let the garlic cool, then squeeze the soft garlic from the cloves into a bowl.

In a small bowl, combine the annatto seeds and 1 cup (240 ml) of room temperature water. Let stand until the seeds turn the water or-ange, about 15 minutes. Strain the liquid into another bowl and discard the seeds.

Using a mortar and pestle or molcajete, combine the roasted garlic with the oregano and pepper and mash into a paste. Measure 1 tablespoon and reserve any extra for another use.

In a blender or food processor, pulse the pepitas until finely ground. Add 1 cup (240 ml) of water and the 1 tablespoon of garlic paste and process until completely blended, about 1 minute.

In a large pot, combine the beans, pepita-roasted garlic mixture, the annatto soaking liquid, 2 cups (480 ml) of water, and the salt. Bring to a boil, reduce the heat and simmer, uncovered, until the beans are soft, about 1 hour. Season with salt. Serve hot topped with red onion and cilantro, and with warm corn tortillas on the side.

INGREDIENT SPOTLIGHT

beans
(black beans)

corn

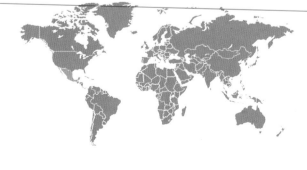

*Carbon Emissions:
CO2e: 0.04*

This meal emits 96.18 percent less carbon than the average meal in the world's highest-emitting countries.

MAKE DO RATATOU(ILLE)

Danielle Nierenberg
United States

2 large imperfect tomatoes, left whole

4 medium bruised tomatoes,
cut into ¼-inch-thick (0.5 cm) slices

4 bruised garlic cloves, minced

½ cup (120 ml) olive oil

1 teaspoon cayenne pepper

Salt and freshly ground black pepper

4 small end-of-season red or green bell peppers, sliced crosswise into ¼-inch-thick (0.5 cm) rings

3 baby eggplants, cut into ¼-inch-thick (0.5 cm) slices

2 medium zucchini that are looking a little tired, cut into ¼-inch-thick (0.5 cm) slices

2 medium red onions on their last legs, cut into ¼-inch-thick (0.5 cm) rings

2 teaspoons fresh rosemary that has been in your refrigerator far too long and needs to be used, finely chopped, plus a rosemary sprig for serving

Rice, couscous, pasta or crusty bread, for serving

Preheat the oven to 350°F (180°C).

Cut the large imperfect tomatoes into chunks and place in a medium bowl. Use the back of a wooden spoon to smash the tomatoes until crushed. Add the garlic, ¼ cup (60 ml) of the olive oil and the cayenne pepper. Season generously with salt and pepper and stir to combine. Spread the tomato sauce on the bottom of a 9 x 13-inch (23 by 33 cm) or similar-sized glass or metal baking dish.

Arrange the sliced tomatoes, bell peppers, eggplants, zucchini and red onion upright in an alternating pattern in tight rows to fill the entire baking dish. Drizzle with the remaining ¼ cup (60 ml) of olive oil, sprinkle with the rosemary and season with salt and pepper. Bake until the vegetables are completely soft and tender, about 2 hours and 30 minutes. Finish with the rosemary sprig and serve with pasta, rice or crusty bread.

INGREDIENT SPOTLIGHT

zucchini

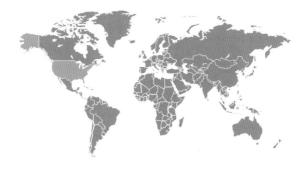

Carbon Emissions:
CO2e: 0.4

This meal emits 61.80 percent less carbon than the average meal in the world's highest-emitting countries.

FONIO AND SWEET POTATO CRAB CAKES

with Spicy Papaya-Lime Sauce

Pierre Thiam
Diola and Fulani Communities
Sénégal

For the crab cakes:

1 large sweet potato (about 1 pound / 450 g), peeled and cut into 2-inch (5 cm) chunks

1 large egg, plus 1 large egg yolk

1 green bell pepper, stemmed, seeded and finely chopped

½ cup (57 g) cooked fonio

¼ cup (34 g) finely ground cornmeal

1 scallion (white part only), chopped

2 tablespoons minced fresh flat-leaf parsley

2 tablespoons fresh lemon juice

2 tablespoons mayonnaise

2 teaspoons Dijon mustard

1 ½ teaspoons ground cumin

1 teaspoon freshly ground pepper

¾ pound (340 g) sustainably sourced lump crabmeat, picked over for cartilage and shells

½ teaspoon salt

⅓ cup (75 ml) vegetable oil

For the papaya-lime sauce:

1 cup (176 g) chopped peeled papaya

½ Scotch bonnet or habanero chili, stemmed, seeded and minced

1 scallion (white and light green parts), chopped

1 tablespoon chopped fresh cilantro (coriander) leaves

1 teaspoon fresh lime juice, plus lime wedges for serving

1 garlic clove, minced

Salt

INGREDIENT SPOTLIGHT

sweet potatoes   **corn**

Make the crab cakes:

Bring a small pot of salted water to a boil. Add the sweet potato chunks, reduce the heat and simmer until tender and easily pierced with a fork, about 12 minutes. Drain the potatoes, place in a large bowl and mash with a fork until smooth. Let cool to room temperature.

Add the egg and egg yolk to the mashed and cooled sweet potatoes and beat with a wooden spoon until fully combined. Stir in the bell pepper, cooked fonio, cornmeal, scallion, parsley, lemon juice, mayonnaise, mustard, cumin and pepper. Fold in the crabmeat. Form the mixture into 12 cakes—they should be about 2 ½ inches (6.25 cm) in diameter and ½ inch (1.25 cm) thick—and sprinkle with the salt. Place on a platter, cover lightly with plastic wrap and refrigerate for at least 1 hour and up to 24 hours.

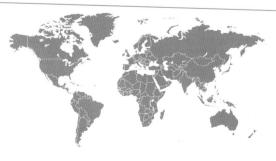

Carbon Emissions: CO2e: 2.81

This meal emits 2.68 times more carbon than the average meal in the world's highest-emitting countries. Be sure the meat you purchase is sustainably sourced.

While the crab cakes are chilling, make the papaya-lime sauce:

In a blender, combine the papaya, Scotch bonnet chili, scallion, cilantro, lime juice, garlic and ¼ teaspoon salt. Process until the ingredients are fully combined but the mixture is still a bit chunky. Transfer to a small bowl, season to taste with salt and set aside.

Cook the crab cakes:

Line a large plate with paper towels.

Heat the vegetable oil in a large skillet over medium heat. Working in two batches, add the crab cakes and cook, flipping once, until golden brown all over, 3 to 4 minutes per side. Transfer to the paper towel–lined plate to drain. Repeat to cook the remaining crab cakes. Serve warm with the sauce and lime wedges on the side.

SOPA DE MILHO

Brazilian Corn Chowder

Denise Browning
Brazil

3 tablespoons vegetable oil

1 large white onion, chopped

4 garlic cloves, minced

6 cups (1.4 liters) low-sodium vegetable broth

1 large potato, peeled and diced

3 ¼ cups (520 g) fresh or frozen sweet corn

Salt and freshly ground black pepper

½ cup (113 g) plain full-fat yogurt

3 tablespoons chopped fresh chives

In a large heavy pot, heat the vegetable oil over medium heat. Add the onion and cook, stirring, until softened and translucent, about 4 minutes. Add the garlic and cook, stirring, for 1 minute. Add the broth, increase the heat to medium-high and bring to a boil. Add the potato and 2 ¼ cups (360 g) of the corn, then reduce the heat and simmer until the potato is tender, 15 to 20 minutes. Season with salt and pepper.

Working in batches as needed, transfer the soup and some of the yogurt to a blender. Place a kitchen towel on top of the blender and carefully blend until creamy. Repeat as needed with the rest of the soup and yogurt. (Alternatively, add the yogurt to the pot of soup and use an immersion blender.) Return the soup to the pot, add the remaining 1 cup (160 g) of corn and cook, stirring occasionally, until the corn is cooked and hot, about 2 minutes. Season generously with salt and pepper. Divide the soup among bowls and garnish with chopped chives.

INGREDIENT SPOTLIGHT

potatoes   corn

Carbon Emissions: CO2e: 0.59

This meal emits 43.64 percent less carbon than the average meal in the world's highest-emitting countries.

KERA NA CUTLETS

Banana Croquettes with Amaranth

Anahita Dhondy

India

4 large unripe (green) bananas (about 2 ¼ pounds / 1 kg total), washed but unpeeled

3 tablespoons sesame oil

5 to 6 hot green chilis, finely chopped

1 (1-inch / 2.5 cm) piece ginger, peeled and grated

1 teaspoon cumin seeds

1 teaspoon ground coriander

½ teaspoon ground turmeric

½ teaspoon ground cumin

2 tablespoons finely chopped fresh mint leaves

2 tablespoons finely chopped fresh cilantro (coriander) leaves

1 cup (200 g) cooked millet

¼ cup (60 ml) fresh lemon juice

Salt

1 cup (200 g) amaranth

Chutney, for serving

Bring a large pot of water to a boil. Add the unpeeled bananas and cook until very soft—the bananas will turn black and the peels may split—about 45 minutes. Remove the bananas and let cool slightly. While still warm, peel and mash the bananas.

In a large frying pan, heat the sesame oil over medium-high heat. Add the green chilis, ginger, cumin seeds, coriander, turmeric and ground cumin, and cook for 1 minute to release the flavors. Add the mashed bananas, stir and cook for 5 to 7 minutes to flavor the banana. Add the fresh mint and cilantro, followed by the cooked millet, and mix to combine. Add the lemon juice, season with salt and remove from the heat. Let cool slightly.

Wet your hands and shape the banana mixture into about 25 croquettes, roughly ½ inch (1.25 cm) in diameter and 2 inches (5 cm) in length.

Preheat the oven to 350°F (180°C).

Heat a deep frying pan over medium-high heat.

Working in batches, add just enough amaranth to cover the bottom of the pan with a single layer. Cover the pan and shake it back and forth over the heat. You should hear the amaranth popping; if you don't, the pan isn't hot enough. As soon as the popping stops—this should take about 8 minutes—transfer the puffed amaranth to a sheet pan and let cool. Repeat as needed to pop all the amaranth. Set aside a small handful of puffed amaranth for serving.

Brush the croquettes with a little water and then roll them in the puffed amaranth and arrange on a sheet pan. Bake until the amaranth forms a crust, 35 to 40 minutes. Sprinkle with the reserved puffed amaranth and serve hot with chutney on the side.

INGREDIENT SPOTLIGHT

bananas

Carbon Emissions
CO2e: 0.48

This meal emits 54.1 percent less carbon than the average meal in the world's highest-emitting countries.

ACKNOWLEDGMENTS

Sara Bond, Editor | Kitchen Connection

Earlene Cruz, Back Matter Author, Editor | Managing Director, Kitchen Connection

H.E. Ambassador José Blanco | The Permanent Mission of the Dominican Republic to the United Nations

H.E. Ambassador Alexander Marschik | The Permanent Mission of Austria to the United Nations

H.E. Ambassador Pio Wennubst, Tim Kränzlein, Rahel Greter, Katharina Jans |
The Permanent Mission of Switzerland to the Food and Agriculture Organization of the United Nations

Alexandra Arias, Minister Counsellor | The Permanent Mission of the Dominican Republic to the United Nations

Brette Williams, K–12 Art Teacher

Carben Burbano, Sandra Hittmeyer, Carlo Luciani, Susan Myers | The School Meals Coalition Team
at the United Nations World Food Programme

Chefs and Culinary Experts: José Andrés, Denise Browning, Rosalia Chay Chuc, Anahita Dhondy,
Danielle Nierenberg, Gunhild Stordalen, Pierre Thiam

Claudia Mansfield LaRue, Counsellor | The Permanent Mission of the Dominican Republic to the United Nations

Dr. Hans Hoogeveen, Advisor | Kitchen Connection

Dr. Rosa Rolle, Team Leader, Food Losses and Waste | Food and Agriculture Organization of the United Nations

Dr. Gunhild Stordalen, Advisor | Kitchen Connection

Edward Bogard, Lorenzo Gentile, Lindsey Hook, Kazuki Kitaoka | World Food Forum

Iain Shepherd | EAT

Jasmin Wanner | The Permanent Mission of Austria to the United Nations

Juliet Kigundu, Team Lead | Coordination Unit, Conference Affairs Division,
United Nations Framework Convention on Climate Change

Laura Lopez, Director of Conference Affairs | United Nations Framework Convention on Climate Change

Lauren Salkeld, Culinary Editor

Sara Farley, Advisor | Kitchen Connection

BETA READERS

Natalia Gabriella Alvez, Sofia Castilblanco, Darlenie Samantha Herrera, Emily Hoey, Abigail Leu, Salma Marzouk,
Ashley Nicole Medina, Justin Moffatt, Diana Nunez, Tereza Ramos

Quentin Angelo Canastra, Middle School Student, Age 11

Sofia Castilblanco, High School Student, Age 18

Samanda Farag, High School Student, Age 14

Sabrina Farag, Middle School Student, Age 10

PARTNERS

EAT

The Kingdom of the Netherlands

The Permanent Mission of Austria to the United Nations

The Permanent Mission of the Dominican Republic to the United Nations

The Permanent Mission of Switzerland to the Food and Agriculture Organizations of the United Nations

The Rockefeller Foundation

The School Meals Coalition

The Union City Board of Education

World Food Forum of the Youth Committee of the Food and Agriculture Organization of the United Nations

FOR PARENTS AND CAREGIVERS

Bean and Bell Pepper Chili with Cauliflower Rice

Total Calories: 420 Grams of Fat: 15g Sodium: 840mg Total Carbohydrates: 59g Sugar: 13g Fiber: 18g Protein: 19g

Fonio and Sweet Potato Crab Cakes with Spicy Papaya-Lime Sauce

Total Calories: 280 Grams of Fat: 9g Sodium: 620mg Total Carbohydrates: 35g Sugar: 3g Fiber: 3g Protein: 16g

Garbanzos con Espinacas (Moorish-Style Chickpea and Spinach Stew)

Total Calories: 370 Grams of Fat: 19g Sodium: 720mg Total Carbohydrates: 41g Sugar: 2g Fiber: 12g Protein: 14g

Kera Na Cutlets (Banana Croquettes with Amaranth)

Total Calories: 630 Grams of Fat: 57g Sodium: 10mg Total Carbohydrates: 30g Sugar: 2g Fiber: 2g Protein: 4g

Make Do Ratatou(ille)

Total Calories: 300 Grams of Fat: 20g Sodium: 840mg Total Carbohydrates: 33g Sugar: 15g Fiber: 9g Protein: 5g

On Sikil Bi Bu'ul (Black Bean Pipian)

Total Calories: 90 Grams of Fat: 1g Sodium: 360mg Total Carbohydrates: 16g Sugar: 0g Fiber: 6g Protein: 6g

Sopa de Milho (Brazilian Corn Chowder)

Total Calories: 320 Grams of Fat: 12g Sodium: 210mg Total Carbohydrates: 50g Sugar: 10g Fiber: 7g Protein: 9g

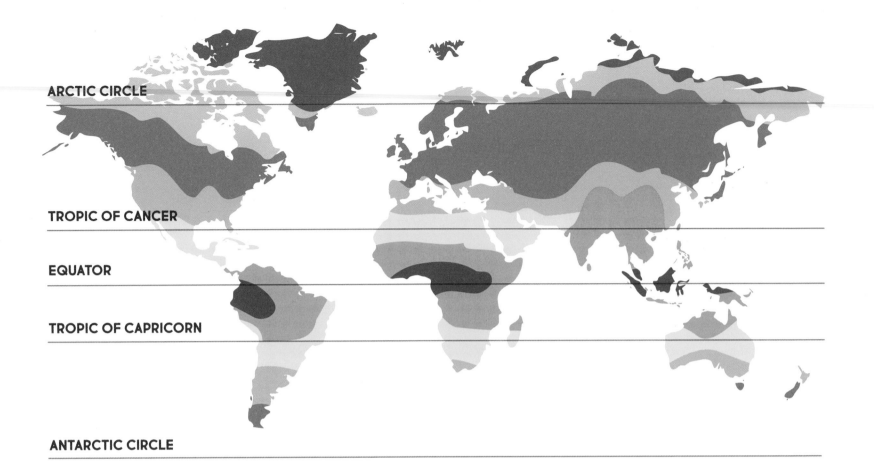

ARCTIC CIRCLE

TROPIC OF CANCER

EQUATOR

TROPIC OF CAPRICORN

ANTARCTIC CIRCLE

CLIMATE ZONES

WHICH FOODS GROW WHERE?

With the effects of climate change, these zones are shifting. While we might be able to grow certain fruits and vegetables in some regions now, as the climate changes, it will be harder to grow those same foods in the future.

Equatorial Zone

Bananas, pineapple, cacao, fonio

Subequatorial Zone

Bananas, pineapple, cacao, beans, chickpeas, corn, broccoli, cauliflower

Tropical Zone

Bananas, pineapple, cacao, avocado, beans, chickpeas, corn, broccoli, cauliflower, strawberries, green beans

Subtropical Zone

Potatoes, avocado, corn, apples, zucchini, green beans, broccoli, cauliflower, strawberries, asparagus

Temperate Zone

Potatoes, apples, corn, beans, green beans, asparagus

Subpolar Zone

Polar Zone